Word for Beginners

M.L. HUMPHREY

TITLES BY M.L. HUMPHREY

WORD ESSENTIALS
Word for Beginners
Intermediate Word

POWERPOINT ESSENTIALS
PowerPoint for Beginners

EXCEL ESSENTIALS
Excel for Beginners
Intermediate Excel
50 Useful Excel Functions

BUDGETING FOR BEGINNERS
Budgeting for Beginners
Excel for Budgeting

WRITING ESSENTIALS
Writing for Beginners
Excel for Writers
Achieve Writing Success

SELF-PUBLISHING ESSENTIALS
Excel for Self-Publishers
AMS Ads for Authors
CreateSpace for Beginners
ACX for Beginners

CONTENTS

INTRODUCTION

The purpose of this guide is to introduce you to the basics of using Microsoft Word. While there are a number of other word processing programs out there, Word is still the gold-standard go-to program in use in large portions of the corporate world, so if you're going to be involved in a white collar job (and even some blue collar jobs), being familiar with Word will be a significant advantage for you. And essential for many jobs. (The days of having an assistant who could do those things for you are gone.)

It's also the program I use for all of my writing. (This book isn't going to be focused on self-publishing, but if you format a document the right way in Word you can publish directly to most of the major sales platforms without any additional effort.)

Word can be incredibly simple to use. At its most basic, you can open a new file, type in your text, save, and be done. But chances are that you'll want more control over what you type and how it looks than that. Maybe you need to use a different font or font size. Maybe you want to indent your paragraphs. Maybe you want to include a bulleted or numbered list in your document.

That's where this guide comes in. I'll walk you through the absolute basics (open, save, delete), too, but most of this guide will be focused on what to do with your text once it's been typed into your document.

Having said that, we're not going to cover everything you can do in Word. The goal of this guide is to get you up to speed and comfortable with what you'll need for probably 98% of what you'll use Word for on a daily basis.

The exceptions to that are if you're working in an environment where you need to use track changes to work on a group document or one where you need to create tables or complex multilevel lists. Those are more advanced topics that are covered in *Intermediate Word*.

The goal here is to give you a solid foundation that you can work from, and I don't want to distract from those core skills by getting into specialized topics that either won't apply to most users or that require enough detail to understand that they'll likely confuse a beginning user.

Another thing to note before we get started. All of the screenshots I'm going to show you are from Word 2013. If you have an earlier version of Word, especially a version prior to 2007, things may look different at the top of the screen. All of the shortcut keys, which I would recommend you use, will be the same, but navigation won't be.

With Excel I recommend that people with older versions upgrade to a post-2007 version of the program. With Word, especially for the beginner level, that probably isn't necessary. However, if you're using a really old version of Word you're going to have less help options. Right now the Microsoft website only has tutorials for Word 2010, 2013, and 2016, and most users won't have access to your version of Word to be able to see what you're seeing.

If you're using Word 2016, nothing we're going to cover here appears to have changed with the most recent version, so you should be fine.

Alright then. Ready? Let's do this.

BASIC TERMINOLOGY

Before we get started, I want to make sure that we're on the same page in terms of terminology.

TAB

I refer to the menu choices at the top of the screen (File, Home, Insert, Design, Page Layout, References, Mailings, Review, View, Developer) as tabs. If you click on one you'll see that the way it's highlighted sort of looks like an old-time filing system.

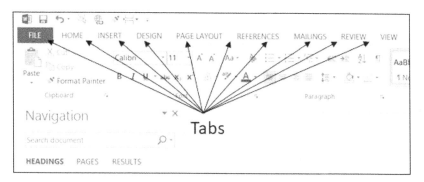

Each tab you select will show you different options. For example, in the image above, I have the Home tab selected and you can do various tasks such as cut/copy/paste, format paint, change the font, change the formatting of a paragraph, apply a style to your text, find/replace words in your document, or select the text in your document. Other tabs give other options.

CLICK

If I tell you to click on something, that means to use your mouse (or trackpad) to move the arrow on the screen over to a specific location and left-click or right-click on the option. (See the next definition for the difference between left-click and right-click).

If you left-click, this selects the item. If you right-click, this generally creates a dropdown list of options to choose from. If I don't tell you which to do, left- or right-click, then left-click.

LEFT-CLICK/RIGHT-CLICK

If you look at your mouse or your trackpad, you generally have two flat buttons to press. One is on the left side, one is on the right. If I say left-click that means to press down on the button on the left. If I say right-click that means press down on the button on the right.

Now, as I sadly learned when I had to upgrade computers and ended up with an HP Envy, not all track pads have the left- and right-hand buttons. In that case, you'll basically want to press on either the bottom left-hand side of the track pad or the bottom right-hand side of the trackpad. Since you're working blind it may take a little trial and error to get the option you want working. (Or is that just me?)

SELECT OR HIGHLIGHT

If I tell you to select text, that means to left-click at the end of the text you want to select, hold that left-click, and move your cursor to the other end of the text you want to select.

Another option is to use the Shift key. Go to one end of the text you want to select. Hold down the shift key and use the arrow keys to move to the other end of the text you want to select. If you arrow up or down, that will select an entire row at a time.

With both methods, which side of the text you start on doesn't matter. You can start at the end and go to the beginning or start at the beginning and go to the end. Just start at one end or the other of the text you want to select.

The text you've selected will then be highlighted in gray. Like the words "sample text" in this image:

This is sample text so you can see what I'm talking about.

If you need to select text that isn't touching you can do this by selecting your first section of text and then holding down the Ctrl key and selecting your second section of text using your mouse. (You can't arrow to the second section of text or you'll lose your already selected text.)

DROPDOWN MENU

If you right-click in a Word document, you will see what I'm going to refer to as a dropdown menu. (Sometimes it will actually drop upward if you're towards the bottom of the document.)

A dropdown menu provides you a list of choices to select from.

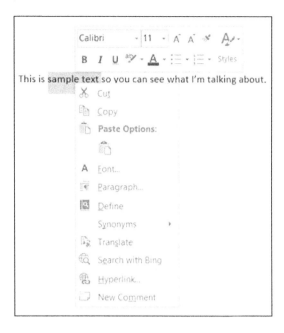

There are also dropdown menus available for some of the options listed under the tabs at the top of the screen. For example, if you go to the Home tab, you'll see small arrows below or next to some of the options, like the numbered list option in the paragraph section. If you click on those arrows, you'll see that there are multiple choices you can choose from listed on a dropdown menu.

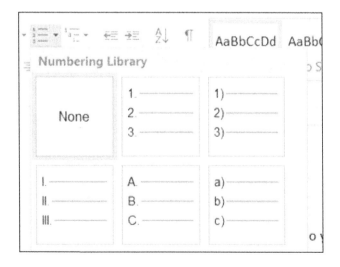

EXPANSION ARROWS

I don't know the official word for these, but you'll also notice at the bottom right corner of most of the sections in each tab that there are little arrows. If you hold your mouse over the arrow it lets you bring up a more detailed set of options, usually through a dialogue box (which we'll discuss next).

In the Home tab, for example, there are expansion arrows for Clipboard, Font, Paragraph, and Styles. Holding your mouse over the arrow will give a brief description of what clicking on the expansion arrow will do.

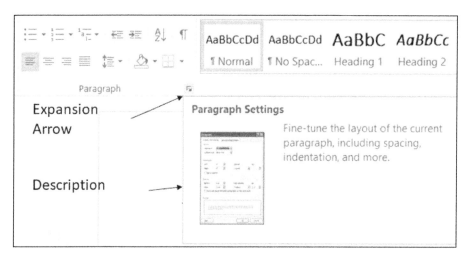

DIALOGUE BOX

Dialogue boxes are pop-up boxes that cover specialized settings. As just mentioned, if you click on an expansion arrow, it will often open a dialogue box that contains more choices than are visible in that section. When you right-click in a Word document and choose Font, Paragraph, or Hyperlink that also opens dialogue boxes. Dialogue boxes allow the most granular level of control over an option

This is the Replace dialogue box.

This may not apply to you, but be aware that if you have more than one Word document open and open a dialogue box in one of those documents, you may not be able to move to the other documents you have open until you close the dialogue box.

SCROLL BAR

This is more useful in Excel than in Word, but on the right-hand side of the screen you should see a scroll bar. You can either click in the space above or below the bar to move up or down a small amount or you can left-click on the bar, hold the left-click, and drag the bar up or down to move through the document more quickly. You can also use the arrows at the top and the bottom to move up and down through your document. (The scroll bar isn't always visible in Word. If you don't see it, move your mouse over to the side of the screen and it should appear.)

In general, you shouldn't see a scroll bar at the bottom of the screen, but it is possible. This would happen if you ever change the zoom level of your document to the point that you're not seeing the entire width of the document in a single screen. (Not something I recommend when working with normal documents.)

ARROW

If I ever tell you to arrow to the left or right or up or down, that just means use your arrow keys. This will move your cursor to the left one space, to the right one space, up one line, or down one line. If you're at the end of a line and arrow to the right, it will take you to the beginning of the next line. If you're at the beginning of a line and arrow to the left, it will take you to the end of the last line.

CURSOR

There are two possible meanings for cursor. One is the one I just used. In your Word document, you will see that there is a blinking line. This indicates where you are in the document. If you type text, each letter will appear where the cursor was at the time you typed it. The cursor will move (at least in the U.S. and I'd assume most European versions) to the right as you type. This version of the cursor should be visible at all times unless you have text selected.

The other type of cursor is the one that's tied to the movement of your mouse or trackpad. When you're typing, it will not be visible. But stop typing and move your mouse or trackpad, and you'll see it. If the cursor is positioned over your text, it will look somewhat like a tall skinny capital I. If you move it up to the menu options or off to the sides, it becomes a white arrow. (Except for when you position it over any option under the tabs that can be typed in such as Font Size or Font where it will once again look like a skinny capital I.)

Usually I won't refer to your cursor, I'll just say, "click" or "select" or whatever action you need to take with it, but moving the cursor to that location will be implied.

QUICK ACCESS TOOLBAR

You might notice that the options in the very top left corner of my version of Word are different from what you see. That's because I've customized the Quick Access Toolbar. You can do this on your version of Word by clicking on the arrow you see at the very end of the list and then checking the commands you want to have available there. It can be useful if there's something you're doing repeatedly (like inserting section breaks) that's located on a different tab than something else you're doing repeatedly (like formatting text).

Of course, it's only useful if you use it. Half the time I forget I've done that. But if you can remember, it's a nice time-saver.

CONTROL SHORTCUTS

Throughout this document, I'm going to mention various control shortcuts that you can use to perform tasks like save, copy, cut, and paste. (There's a list of the most important ones in the appendix.) Each of these will be written as Ctrl + a capital letter, but when you use the shortcut on your computer you don't need to use the capitalized version of the letter. For example, holding down the Ctrl key and the s key at the same time will save your document. I'll write this as Ctrl + S, but that just means hold down the key that says ctrl and the s key at the same time.

ABSOLUTE BASICS

Before we do anything else, there are a few absolute basics that we should cover.

STARTING A NEW WORD FILE

To start a brand new Word file, I click on Word 2013 from my applications menu or the shortcut I have on my computer's taskbar. If you're already in Word and want to open a new Word file, go to the File tab and choose New from the left-hand menu.

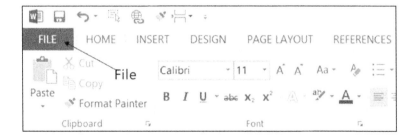

Whichever option you choose will bring up a list of various templates, including the first option which is for a "Blank document". Ninety-nine percent of the time that's the one you'll want. To use it, left-click on the image.

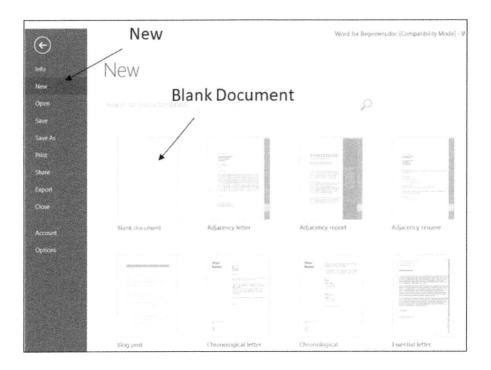

OPENING AN EXISTING WORD FILE

To open an existing Word file you can either go to the folder where the file is saved and double-click on the file name, or (if Word is already open) go to the File tab and choose Open from the left-hand menu. Or you can just open Word without selecting a file and it will provide a list of recent documents to choose from on the left-hand side.

If you're in Word and the document you need is listed, left-click on it once and it will open as long as you haven't renamed the file or moved it since it was last open. (In that case, you'll need to navigate to where the file is saved and open it that way, either through Word or outside of Word.)

To navigate to the file you need, click on Open Other Documents and then click on Computer under Open (if you just opened Word and don't have any files open) or click on Computer under Home (if you already had a file open).

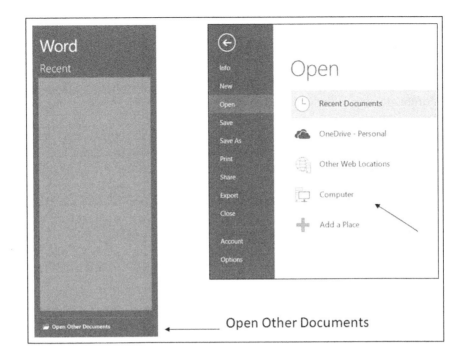

This should give you a list of recent folders you've used or you can click on Browse if the file you need isn't in one of those folders. When you click on Browse this will bring up the Open dialogue box (below). From there you can navigate to any location on your computer.

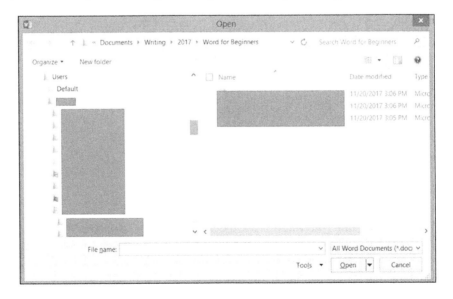

SAVING A WORD FILE

To quickly save a document, you can use Ctrl + S or click on the small image of a floppy disk in the top left corner of the screen above File. For a document you've already saved that will overwrite the prior version of the document with the current version and will keep the file name, file type, and file location the same.

If you try to save a file that has never been saved before, it will automatically default to the Save As option which requires that you specify where to save the file, give it a name, and designate the file type. There are defaults for name and format, but you'll want to change the name of the document to something better than Document2.

You can also choose Save As when you want to change the location of a file, the name of a file, or the file type. (With respect to file type, I sometimes need to, for example, save a .doc file as a .pdf file or a .doc file as a .docx file for use with certain formatting programs.)

The first choice you have to make for Save As is where you want to save the file. I see a list of my most recent six folders listed and can also choose to Browse if I want to use a different location than one of the folders listed.

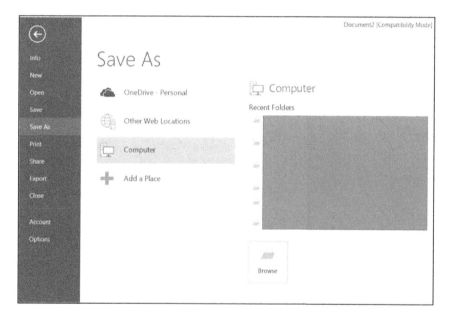

When you click on the location where you want to save the file, this will bring up the Save As dialogue box. Type in the name you want for the file and choose the file type. My file type defaults to Word 97-2003 Document (.doc) which is the format I prefer to save in because it's the easiest format for all users and all versions of Word to open. If you save as a .docx file you may encounter situations where someone you share the file with won't be able to open it.

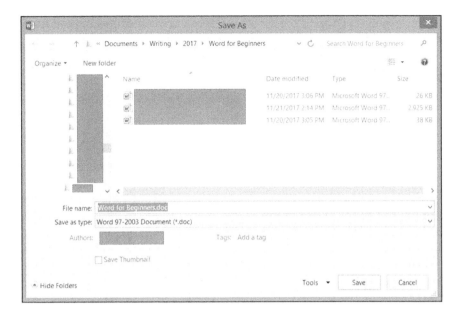

If you had already saved the file and you choose to Save As but keep the same location, name, and format as before, Word will overwrite the previous version of the file just like it would have if you'd used Save.

If you just want to rename a file, it's actually best to close the file and then go to where the file is saved and rename it that way rather than use Save As. Using Save As will keep the original of the file as well as creating the newer version. That's great when you want version control (which I often need), but not when you just wanted to rename your file from Great Book Version 22 to Great Book FINAL.

RENAMING A WORD FILE

As discussed above, you can use Save As to give an existing file a new name, but that approach will leave you with two versions of the file, one with the old name and one with the new name. If you just want to change the name of the existing file, close it and then navigate to where you've saved it. Click on the file name once to select it, click on it a second time to highlight the name, and then type in the new name you want to use, replacing the old one. If you rename the file this way outside of Word, there will only be one version of the file left, the one with the new name you wanted.

Just be aware that if you rename a file by navigating to where it's located and changing the name you won't be able to access the file from the Recent Workbooks listing under Open file, since that will still list the old name which no longer exists.

DELETING A WORD FILE

You can't delete a Word file from within Word. You need to close the file you want to delete and then navigate to where the file is stored and delete the file there without opening it. Once you've located the file, click on the file name. (Only enough to select it. Make sure you haven't double-clicked and highlighted the name which will delete the file name but not the file.) Next, choose

Delete from the menu at the top of the screen, or right-click and choose Delete from the dropdown menu.

CLOSING A WORD FILE

To close a Word file click on the X in the top right corner or go to File and then choose Close. (You can also use Ctrl + W, but I never have.)

If no changes have been made to the document since you saved it last, it will just close.

If changes have been made, Word should ask you if you want to save those changes. You can either choose to save them, not save them, or cancel closing the document and leave it open. I almost always default to saving any changes. If I'm in doubt about whether I'd be overwriting something important, I cancel and choose to Save As and save the current file as a later version of the document just in case (e.g., Great Book v2).

If you had copied an image or a large block of text, you may also have a box pop up asking if you want to keep that image or text when you close the document. Usually the answer to this is no, but if you had planned on pasting that image or text somewhere else and hadn't yet done so, you can say to keep it on the clipboard.

BASIC TASKS

At its most basic, adding text into a Word document is incredibly simple. You simply open a new document and start typing. When you're done, you save the document.

Go ahead and do it. See? Open. Type. Save. Voila.

But you probably want to do more with your text than that. And we'll cover all the formatting, which is the majority of what you'll want to do, in the next section. First, I want to cover a few basic functions that you can perform in Word that will make your life easier as you enter your text and then edit it.

UNDO

Undo lets you take the last thing (or few things) you did, and undo it. That means you don't have to be afraid to try something that you're not sure will work, because you can always reverse it.

To undo something, simply type Ctrl + Z. If you did a few things you didn't like, just keep typing Ctrl + Z until they're all gone. But beware that Word undoes things in order, so if you want to undo the second-to-last thing you did, you'll have to first undo the last thing you did.

REDO

If you take it too far and undo too much and want something back, then you can choose to redo. That's done by typing Ctrl + Y. Go ahead and try it out. Type a sentence in your document. Undo it with Ctrl + Z and then redo it with Ctrl + Y. Easy peasy.

(If you don't want to use control keys, you can also add undo and redo to the Quick Access Toolbar, but I'd highly recommend that you memorize these two. You'll work much faster if you can memorize the control key shortcuts for undo, redo, save, copy, cut, and paste.)

DELETE

Another basic task you need to master is how to delete text. There are a few ways to do this. If you're trying to delete something that you just typed, use the backspace key to delete the letters one at a time.

You can also place the cursor next to the text you want to delete and then use the backspace or delete keys, depending on where the cursor is relative to the text you're trying to delete. If your cursor is on the left-hand side of text, use the delete key. On the right-hand side, use the backspace key. (And if you get it wrong, remember that you have Ctrl + Z to undo what you just did.)

If you want to delete a large chunk of text at one time, select the text you want to delete and then use the delete OR backspace key.

SELECT ALL

The other basic task that you should know about before we start talking formatting is how to select all of the text in your document.

Select All is very useful for applying a format to your entire document. I tend to write in the default font that Word uses and then change the font once I'm done. It's also handy if you want to copy the contents of one document into another. Say, for example, you worked on a group project and each person wrote their individual piece in a separate document and now you need to combine them. Or, like me, you wrote your first novel using separate files for each chapter (Don't do that, by the way.) You can take those final documents, select all, copy, and paste into one master document that combines them.

To Select All, go to the Home tab and then to the Editing section on the far right-hand side and click on the arrow next to Select. In the dropdown menu choose Select All.

Another option is to use Ctrl + A, although I don't consider this one of the control shortcuts that I use often enough to memorize.

I've also added Select All as one of my Quick Access Toolbar options.

If you ever choose all of the text in a document and then decide you didn't want to, just click somewhere in the document and the selection will go away. (You can also arrow up or down, but that will take you to the top or the bottom of the document and you may not want that.)

COPYING, CUTTING, AND PASTING

Copy and Cut are similar. They're both a way to move text from one location to another. Copy leaves the text where it was and creates a copy of that text to move to the new location. Cut removes the text from where it was and puts the text on a "clipboard" (that's usually not visible to you) for movement to a new location.

Paste is how you tell Word where that new location is.

The first step in copying or cutting text is to select all of the text you want to move. To select text you can left-click on one side of the text, hold down that left-click and move your mouse or trackpad until all of the text you want is highlighted. Or you can use the shift key and the arrow keys to select your text.

Once your text is selected, to copy it type Ctrl + C or to cut it type Ctrl + X.

If you don't want to use the control shortcuts, you can also go to the Home tab and in the Clipboard section choose Copy or Cut from there. Or you can right-click after you've selected your text and choose Copy or Cut from the dropdown menu.

I recommend using the control shortcuts, because it's the fastest and these three commands are ones you'll use often enough to make it worth memorizing them.

If you copy text, it remains visible in the location you copied it from. Behind the scenes Word has taken a copy of that text and placed it on a "clipboard" for use elsewhere.

If you cut text, the text is immediately removed from the document. It too is placed on a "clipboard" for use elsewhere. (This also means that cut text, if you choose not to paste it somewhere else, is deleted text.)

To see the clipboard where the items you've copied or cut are stored, go to the Home tab and click on the expansion arrow next to Clipboard. This will bring up a Clipboard display with all of the items you've recently copied or cut from your document.

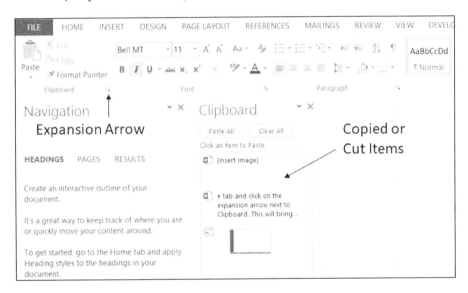

As you can see here, I copied two snippets of text as well as took a screenshot. I could use this clipboard to paste all of those items into my document at once using that Paste All option. (This wasn't always an available option in Word so if you have a really old version you won't be able to see or do this.)

You can also just click on one of the items and it will paste into your document. This can come in handy if you have something you need to paste more than once into your document, but usually you won't need this. You'll just want to copy or cut one item and then paste it into another spot in your document (or another document) right then.

The simplest way to paste something you've just copied or cut is to use Ctrl + V. Simply copy or cut your item, go to where you want to place it, type Ctrl + V, and you're done.

Your other two options are to go to the Clipboard section of the Home tab and click on Paste. Or you can right-click and choose one of the Paste options from the dropdown menu in the document.

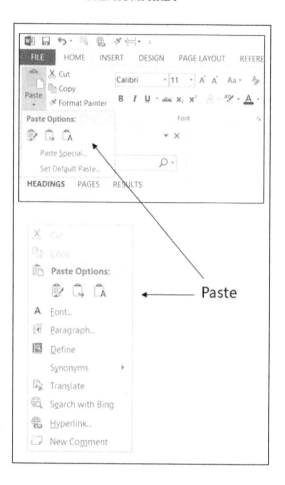

PASTE OPTIONS

If you use Ctrl + V to paste text, you'll be pasting not only the text you copied or cut, but its formatting as well. Usually, that's fine and you'll probably be able to use Ctrl + V ninety-five percent of the time. (And even if you don't want to keep the formatting, there's a trick I'll show you later—using the Format Painter—that you can use to quickly correct formatting after you paste the text into its new location. All it requires is that you have some text that's already formatted the way you want.)

But sometimes you'll want to paste the text in without that formatting. That's where using the Paste dropdown menus comes in handy, because they allow you to choose how you paste your item.

As you can see in the images above, once you've copied or cut an item, you'll be given three paste options: Keep Source Formatting, Merge Formatting, and Keep Text Only. (They're represented by small images, but if you hold your mouse over each one, you'll be able to see the labels.)

In the image below I've pasted the red and bolded word TEST written in Calibri font into a sentence written in black font in Times New Roman using each paste option. This shows how text in a different color, font, and bolding is handled under each paste option.

TEST

Ctrl + V (Paste)

Sample TEST text for demonstration purposes.

Keep Source Formatting

Sample TEST text for demonstration purposes.

Merge Formatting

Sample **TEST** text for demonstration purposes.

Keep Text Only

Sample TEST text for demonstration purposes.

Using Ctrl + V, the color, font, and bolding of the original text remain.

Using Keep Source Formatting gives the same result. Color, font, and bolding are the same as the original text.

With Merge Formatting the color and font of the original text are lost, but the bolding of the original text is not. So "TEST" is now in Times New Roman and black, but it's still bolded.

Using Keep Text Only the color, font, and bolding of the original text are all lost and replaced with the color, font, and bolding (in this case none) of the destination text.

That may seem a little confusing, and honestly, my recommendation is to just use Ctrl + V and fix the formatting after the text is in your document. The main time I use these other paste options is when copying from websites that use hyperlinks that I don't want to bring into my document. Then I paste using Keep Text Only.

If you remember anything from what we just walked through, remember this:

Ctrl + C to copy.

Ctrl + X to cut.

Ctrl + V to paste.

TEXT FORMATTING

Now that you know how to create a file, enter the text you want, and save your work, it's time to actually format that text. Let's start with font.

CHOOSING A FONT – GENERAL THOUGHTS

The font you use governs the general appearance of the text in your document. My version of Word uses Calibri font as the default, but there are hundreds of fonts you can choose. Here is a sample of a few of those choices:

> **Sans-Serif Font Examples:**
>
> Calibri
>
> Arial
>
> Gill Sans MT
>
>
> **Serif Font Examples:**
>
> Times New Roman
>
> Garamond
>
> Palatino Linotype

The first three samples are sans-serif fonts. (That just means they don't have little feet at the bottom of the letters.) The second three samples are serif fonts. (They do have those little feet at the bottom of each letter.) All of these fonts are the same size, but you can see that the different fonts have a different appearance and take up different amounts of space on the page. Arial is darker and taller than Calibri, for example.

Many companies and teachers will specify the font you need to use. If they don't I'd suggest using a serifed font like Garamond or Times New Roman for text since serifed fonts are supposed to be easier to read.

And unless you're working on a creative project, don't get too fancy with your fonts. The six listed in that example above should cover almost any text needs you have. At the end of the day, the goal is for someone to be able to read what you've written. So no Algerian in many body text. Save those fonts for embellishments and section labels.

CHANGING THE FONT

There are a few ways you can change the font in your document. If you already know you want to use a different font, it's easiest to do so before you start typing. Otherwise you'll need to select all of the text you want to change. (Either with Select All if it's all text in the document or by selecting chunks of text and changing them one chunk at a time.)

The first way to change the font is to go to the Font section of the Home tab. Click on the arrow to the right of the current font name and choose from the dropdown menu.

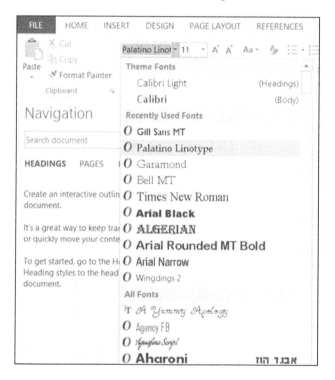

The first section of the dropdown menu lists the fonts for the theme you're using. Usually that'll be the defaults for Word, in this case, Calibri and Calibri Light. Next you'll see Recently Used Fonts. Most of the time there will only be one or two fonts here, but I had used a number recently.

Finally, you'll see a list of all available fonts in alphabetical order. If you know the font you want, you can start typing in its name rather than scroll through the entire list. Otherwise, use the scroll bar on the right-hand side to move through the list. Each font is written using the font to give you an idea what it will look like. See in the example the difference between Algerian and Garamond?

The next way to change your font is to right-click and choose Font from the dropdown menu. This will bring up the Font dialogue box. In the top left corner you can choose the font you want.

There's a third option for changing the font, something I'm going to call the mini formatting menu, in the newest versions of Word. To see this menu, right-click in your document or select a section of text using your mouse. When you select a section of text, a smaller version of the Font section of the Home tab will appear just above your text. If you right-click it will appear above the dropdown menu.

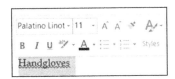

As you can see, one of the options that you can change in the mini formatting menu is the font. (If the font name box is empty, that's because you have text selected and there's more than one font in the selection.) To change the font, click on the arrow to the right of the listed font and choose the one you want from the dropdown just like you would in the Font section of the Home tab. I would recommend that you only use this option for a selection of text that you want to change to a new font. It's much better to change the font for your document in the Home tab.

FONT SIZE

Font size dictates how large the text will be. Here are some examples of different font sizes:

8 pt   12 pt   16 pt

As you can see, the larger the font size, the larger the text. Most documents are written in a ten, eleven, or twelve point font size. Often footnotes or endnotes will use eight or nine point. Chapter headings or title pages will use the larger font sizes. Whatever font size you do use, try to be consistent between different sections of your document. So all main body text should use just one font size. Same for chapter or section headings.

Changing the font size works much the same way as changing the font. You have the same three options: You can go to the Font section of the Home tab, bring up the mini formatting menu by right-clicking, or bring up the Font dialogue box by right-clicking and choosing Font from the dropdown menu. If you want to change existing text, you need to select the text first. If you want to change the font size for text that you're going to type, do so with the Home tab or the Font dialogue box options.

For all three options the font size is listed to the right of the font name.

For the Home tab or mini formatting menu options, you can click on the arrow next to the current font size to bring up a dropdown menu that lets you choose your font size. In the Font dialogue box that list of choices is already visible.

If the font size you want isn't listed, you can type it in instead. Just click into the box for font size and change the number to the font size you want to use.

In the Home tab and the mini formatting menu, if you're only changing the font by one or two point sizes, you can instead use the increase and decrease font options directly to the right of the font size. These are depicted as the letter A with a small arrow above it. The one on the left is an arrow that points upward (to increase the font size). The one on the right is an arrow that points downward (to decrease the font size). If you use the increase/decrease font options, they increase and decrease the font size one place according to the font sizes listed in the dropdown menu.

Here is an image of all three choices for changing font size in the Home tab.

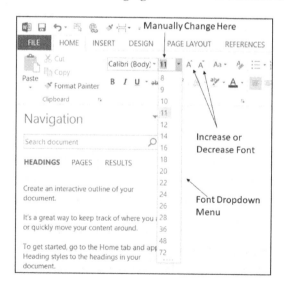

FONT COLOR

Changing your font color works the same as changing your font or font size. Select the text you want to change and then either go to the Font section of the Home tab, pull up the mini formatting menu, or right-click and choose Font from the dropdown menu to bring up the Font dialogue box. This time, though, you want to click on the arrow next to the A with the solid colored line under it in the bottom right corner of the section:

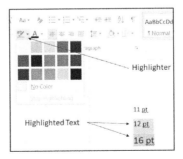

This will give you a dropdown menu with seventy different colors to choose from. Click on the color you want and it will change your text to that color.

If those seventy choices are not enough, you can click on More Colors at the bottom of the dropdown box. This will bring up the Colors dialogue box where you can choose from even more colors or specify a specific color in the Custom tab using RGB values. (Not likely to be needed for a font color, but this does come into play for fill color and is discussed in more detail in *Intermediate Word*.)

HIGHLIGHTING TEXT

Another thing you can do is highlight text in a document much like you might do with a highlighter. You can do this from the Font section of the Home tab or in the mini formatting menu. Select the text you want to highlight and then look for the letters ab and what looks like a pen running diagonally right to left between the ab and a colored line:

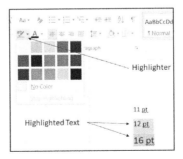

If you want to highlight using the color shown in the line, you can just click on the image. If you want to use a different color, left-click on the arrow and select your color from the dropdown menu.

If you ever highlight text and want to remove the highlight, you can do so by selecting that text, going to the highlight dropdown, and choosing the "no color" option.

Once you've used the highlighter it will show the last color you used as the default color until you close the file. (This carries across documents. I have three documents open at the moment and all three of them now show "no color" as the highlighter option even though I only used it in the one document.)

BOLDING TEXT

This is one you will use often. At least I do. The easiest way to bold text is to use Ctrl + B. You can use it before you start typing the text you want to bold or on a selection of text that you've chosen. For text that is already bolded, you can remove the bolding by selecting the text and using Ctrl + B as well. If you select text that is both bolded and not bolded, you'll need to type Ctrl + B twice, once to bold all of the text and once to remove it.

If you don't want to use the control keys, you can also go to the Font Section of the Home tab and click on the B on the left-hand side. It works the exact same way as using Ctrl + B. If you click on it and then type text that text will be bolded. Or you can select the text you want to bold and then click on the B. To turn off or remove bolding, click on the B again.

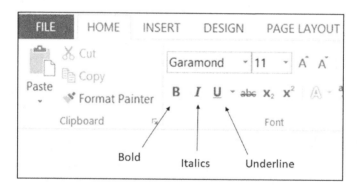

The final option is to select your text, right-click, choose Font from the dropdown menu, and then choose to Bold in the Font Style section of the Font dialogue box. (If you want to both bold and italicize text, you would choose Bold Italic.)

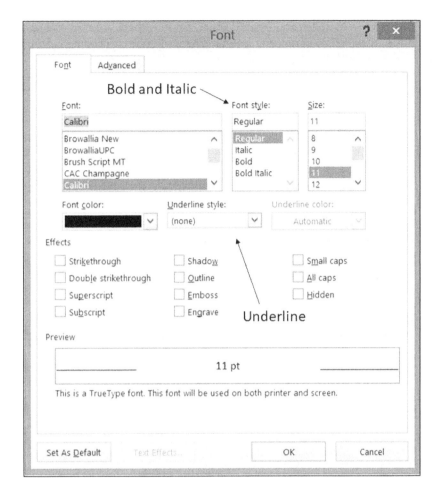

ITALICIZING TEXT

To place text into italics—that means to have it sloped to the side *like this*—the easiest way is to use Ctrl + I. It works the exact same way as bolding text. You can do it before you type the letters or select the text and then use it. And to remove italics, just select the text, and then type Ctrl + I until the italics are gone.

Or in the Font section of the Home tab, you can click on the slanted capital I. And if you use the Font dialogue box, italics are listed under Font Styles. (See the images above in the Bolding section.)

UNDERLINING TEXT

Underlining text works much the same way as bolding or italicizing text. The control keys you'll need to use are Ctrl + U and in the Font section of the Home tab the underline option is represented by an underlined U. (See image above in the Bolding section.)

Underline is different from italics and bold, though, because there are multiple underline options to choose from. Using Ctrl + U will provide a single line underline of your text. So will just clicking on the U in the Font section of the Home tab.

But if you click on the arrow next to the U in the Font section, you will see seven additional underline options you can choose from.

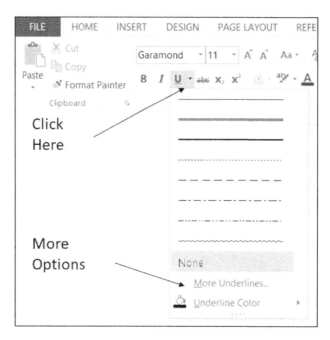

Choosing More Underlines at the bottom of that list of options will open the Font dialogue box where you will have a total of seventeen underline styles to choose from. You can also go direct to the Font dialogue box by selecting your text and then right-clicking and choosing Font from the dropdown. But, honestly, while it's good to know those other options are there the basic single underline will be all you need most of the time so if you remember anything remember Ctrl +U.

REMOVING BOLDING, UNDERLINING, OR ITALICS

I touched on this briefly above, but let's go over it again.

If you have bolded, underlined, or italicized text and you want to remove that formatting, you can simply select the text and use the command in question to remove that formatting type. So Ctrl + B, I, or U or click on the letter in the Font section of the Home tab or go to the Font dialogue box and remove the formatting from there.

If you select text that is partially formatted one way and partially formatted another—so say half of it is bolded and half is not—you may need to use the command twice. The first time will apply the formatting to all of the selected text, the second time will remove it from all of the selected text.

Also, with specialty underlining (all but the default, first choice), using Ctrl + U once will revert the type of underlining to the basic single underline. To remove the underline altogether, you'll need to use Ctrl + U a second time.

COPYING FORMATTING

There are going to be times where you've already formatted part of your document or you have a document that's formatted in the way you want and you want to "copy" that formatting to another portion of your document or a different document. This is where the Format Painter tool comes in handy. It's located on the Home tab in the Clipboard section.

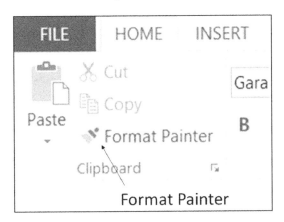

We have yet to discuss formatting paragraphs, but it's really useful when it comes to that because it will copy not only basic formatting like the font, font size, color, bolding, underline, italics, etc. but also the paragraph spacing and indent. Often in my corporate career I was able to use the format painter to fix a document when nothing else worked.

If you want to take formatting from one set of text and use it on another, first select the text with the formatting you want. Next, click on the Format Painter image. Finally, select the text you want to copy the formatting to.

A few tips.

You need to use the mouse or trackpad to select the text you want to have the formatting. Using the arrow and shift keys doesn't work.

You'll know that the format painter is ready to paint the format when you see a little paintbrush next to your cursor as you hover over your document.

You can sweep formatting that's in one document to another document.

Format painting can be unreliable if there are different formats in the sample you're taking the formatting from. For example, if I have a sample where part of the text is red and part of the text is bolded and I format sweep from that sample to new text, only the formatting of the first letter in my sample will carry over.

Sometimes with paragraph or numbered list formatting, I have to select the paragraph from the bottom to the top instead of top to bottom in order to get the format painter to carry over the formatting I want. And sometimes I need to select more than one paragraph to sweep from in order to get the line spacing to carry over.

Last but not least, when you copy formatting over, all of the formatting in your target text will be removed. This can be an issue if you've used italics or bolding within a paragraph, for example. Maybe you want the paragraph spacing and font and font size from another document so you use the format painter. Problem is, any bold, italics, or underline in the text you're copying the formatting to will be lost.

We'll talk about how to do this later, but there is a way in newer versions of Word to find all italicized text in a document. Same with bolded or underlined. So you could format sweep and then go back to a prior version of the document, locate the italics, bolding, and underlining, and manually put them back into the document now that it has the new formatting. It all depends on which option will be easier.

In summary, while the format painter is incredibly powerful and I use it all the time, you also need to be cautious in how you apply it so that you don't inadvertently introduce errors or erase formatting you don't want to erase. Sometimes it's the only way I can get paragraphs to look the same. Nothing else will do it. So learn this tool. It *will* save you at some point or another.

PARAGRAPH FORMATTING

That was basic text formatting. Now it's time to cover paragraph formatting. This is where you set the indent for a paragraph or make sure that it's double-spaced or that there's enough separation between paragraphs.

In this guide we're going to walk through how to change the formatting of a specific paragraph. Once you're comfortable enough in Word, I'd advise that you learn Styles and use those instead. We're not going to cover them in this guide because to really use them well you need to create customized Styles which is beyond a beginner-level skill. I will touch on a few points about Styles at the end of this chapter, though, and they are covered in *Intermediate Word* if you reach the point you want to learn about them. (Also, at the end of this guide I'll point you towards other resources you can use to learn what isn't covered here.)

Alright then. Let's talk about how to format a paragraph one element at a time.

PARAGRAPH ALIGNMENT

There are four choices for paragraph alignment. Left, Center, Right, and Justified. In the image below I've taken the same three-line paragraph and applied each alignment style to it:

This paragraph is **left-aligned**. I now need to add enough text to this paragraph to make more than one line so you can see the difference between the different alignments. Good times. Especially since I need at least three lines each for you to really see this.

This paragraph is **centered**. I now need to add enough text to this paragraph to make more than one line so you can see the difference between the different alignments. Good times. Especially since I need at least three lines each for you to really see this.

This paragraph is **right-aligned**. I now need to add enough text to this paragraph to make more than one line so you can see the difference between the different alignments. Good times. Especially since I need at least three lines each for you to really see this.

This paragraph is **justified**. I now need to add enough text to this paragraph to make more than one line so you can see the difference between the different alignments. Good times. Especially since I need at least three lines each for you to really see this.

Left-aligned, the first example, is how you'll often see text in documents. The text is lined up along the left-hand side of the page and allowed to end in a jagged line on the right-hand side of the page.

Justified, the last example, is the other common way for text to be presented. Text is still aligned along the left-hand side, but instead of leaving the right-hand side ragged, Word adjusts the spacing between words so that all lines are also aligned along the right-hand side.

For school papers and most work documents you're probably going to use left-alignment. Some places may prefer justified. Books are often published with justified but many do use left-aligned.

Centered, the second example, is rarely used for full paragraphs of text like the main body text of a book. It can be used for sections of text that are only a few lines long such as a quote that starts a chapter. Also, it's often used for chapter or section titles that are then centered over left-aligned or justified text. As you can see, it centers each line and distributes the text for that line equally to the left and right of the center point.

Right-aligned, the third example, is rare. It aligns all of the text along the right-hand side and leaves the left-hand side ragged. I have seen it used for text in side margins of non-fiction books and would expect to see it used for languages that read right to left.

Now that you understand the difference between the options, how do you change the paragraph alignment of your text? As with font, you can do this either before you start typing or by selecting text you've already typed. (For just one paragraph, you can click anywhere in the paragraph, you don't need to select the whole paragraph.)

The way I change paragraph alignment is by going to the Paragraph section of the Home tab and clicking on the image for the alignment type I need in the bottom row of that section.

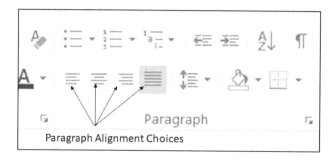

Paragraph Alignment Choices

Each image contains lines that show that type of alignment, but you can also hold your mouse over each one and Word will tell you which one it is.

There are also control shortcuts. Ctrl + L will left-align, Ctrl + E will center your text, Ctrl + R will right-align, and Ctrl + J will justify it. The only one of these I use enough to have memorized is Ctrl + E. I either use left-alignment, which is the default, or I use a Style that includes justifying the text. Since centering is something you do with section headers, I do use that one fairly often.

The third way to change your paragraph alignment is to right-click in your document and choose Paragraph from the dropdown menu. This will give you the Paragraph dialogue box. The first option within that box is a dropdown where you can choose the alignment type you want.

PARAGRAPH SPACING

If you've ever attended school in the United States, you've probably been told at some point to submit a five-page paper that's double-spaced with one inch margins. Or if you've ever submitted a short story you were told to use a specific line spacing. So how do you do that?

As with the other formatting options, you can either do this before you start typing or by selecting the paragraphs you want to change after they've been entered into the document.

Once you're ready, go to the Paragraph section of the Home tab and locate the Line and Paragraph Spacing option. It's to the right of the paragraph alignment options and looks like five lines of text with two big blue arrows on the left-hand side, one pointing up, one pointing down. Click on the small black arrow to the right of the image to bring up the dropdown menu.

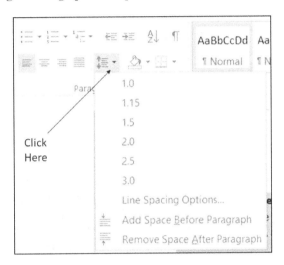

You'll see that you have a choice of single-spaced (1.0) or double-spaced (2.0) as well as 1.15, 1.5, 2.5, and 3.0 spacing. If you want a different spacing than one of those options, then click on Line Spacing Options at the bottom of the list to bring up the Paragraph dialogue box. There you can enter an exact number or choose from even more options. Generally, the dropdown will be sufficient, though.

Another option, of course, is to just go straight to the Paragraph dialogue box by right-clicking and choosing Paragraph from the dropdown menu. (Just remember to have already selected the text you want to change or to change the spacing before you start typing.)

BULLETED LISTS

A bulleted list is just what it sounds like, a list of items where each line starts with a bullet mark on the left-hand side. The most common bullet choice is probably a small dark black circle that's filled in, but Word has a few options you can choose from:

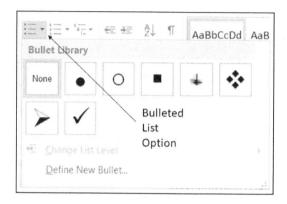

To create a bulleted list, go to the Paragraph section of the Home tab and click on the bulleted list dropdown menu to select the type of bullet you want to use in your list.

If you know that what you're about to type is going to be a bulleted list, you can click on the bulleted list option before you start typing. Word will insert the bullet you've chosen and move the cursor to where your text will start.

If you've already typed the first row of text that you want bulleted, you can click on the bulleted list option you want while in that row of text and it will convert it to the first entry of a bulleted list.

Hitting enter at the end of the line in a bulleted list, will start a new line with a bullet.

Or, last but not least, if all of your text has already been entered you can select all of the lines that you want to be part of the bulleted list and then choose the bulleted list option and it should convert your text to a bulleted list with one bullet per paragraph or individual line.

If you have a line that's bulleted and you don't want it to be, you can go to the beginning of the text on that line and backspace. Once will remove the bullet. Twice will move the text to the beginning of the line. Or, you can select the line and choose None from the bulleted list dropdown menu.

(You can also use the Format Painter to apply bullets to a list of entries or to remove them depending on the formatting of your source data.)

Another way to create a bulleted list is to select your text and then right-click to bring up the mini formatting menu. The bulleted list dropdown is one of the available options.

With bulleted lists, Word automatically indents your text. If you don't want that, you can use the Decrease Indent option (discussed below) to move the text back to the left-hand side of the page but keep the bullets.

NUMBERED LISTS

You can also create a "numbered" list that uses letters or numbers for each entry in your list instead of bullets.

One easy way to create a numbered list in more recent versions of Word is to simply type the first number you want to use, the separator mark you want, and then a space. Word will automatically indent that entry and turn it into the first entry in a numbered list. So, for example, I might type the number 1 followed by a period and then a space. Word will indent that 1. and make it the first entry in my list. This works with all of the options on the dropdown menu we're about to look at. (This is part of the Autocorrect settings, so a little thunderbolt will appear next to the number when this first happens. If you don't want that to happen, you can click on the arrow next to the thunderbolt and have Word reverse the change by telling it to Undo Automatic Numbering.)

When you hit enter after typing in the text for your first line, Word will continue the numbering you started.

The other option, especially if you already have your list and just need to convert it to a numbered list, is to select the lines you want to number, go to the Home tab and in the Paragraph section click on the arrow next to the Numbering option and choose the numbered list option you want from there.

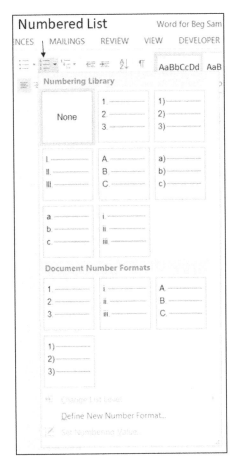

As you can see, you have the option to choose between lists that use 1, 2, 3 or i, ii, iii or A, B, C or a, b, c, or I, II, III and then between using a period after the "number" or a paren. For a basic list, this should be all you really need.

When you right-click on your list you'll also see that the mini formatting menu is available and that one of the options is the numbering option. So instead of going to the Home tab, you could just right-click and choose from there to create your numbered list.

You can also create two-level or three-level lists by using the tab key to indent your numbering or the shift-tab key to decrease the indent on your numbering. This gives you, for example, a first level that is 1, 2, 3 with the option of a second level under that that's a, b, c. To do this, go to each line you want to be second-level (or third-level) and use the tab key to indent that line. This will change the numbering of the line at the same time it moves it inward.

If you need very fine control over a multi-level list or you need a list that works throughout your document and has lots of breaks in it, you'll probably want to use an option we're not going to cover here called the Multilevel List option. (It's the option to the right of the number list option in the Paragraph section.) I discuss that option in *Intermediate Word*, but I'll tell you now that it's incredibly finicky to use and one of the things I hate most in Word.

Back to basic numbered lists. If you had a numbered list earlier in your document and want that numbering to continue in the location where you are now, you can do that. Or, if Word continued the numbering and you wanted it to start over at 1, you can do that, too. In either case, you're going to right-click on the number you want to change. You'll then either choose Continue Numbering (to continue from a prior section) or Set Numbering Value (to change the value you start with back to 1 or A or whatever you're using).

INDENTING AN ENTIRE PARAGRAPH OR LIST

Now that we've talked about lists, let's talk about increasing or decreasing an indent. When you're dealing with paragraphs, the best way to do this is in the Paragraph dialogue box. Right-click on your paragraph and from the dropdown menu choose Paragraph. Once the Paragraph dialogue box opens, you can set the indent for the entire paragraph as well as whether the paragraph will have a special indent only for the first line.

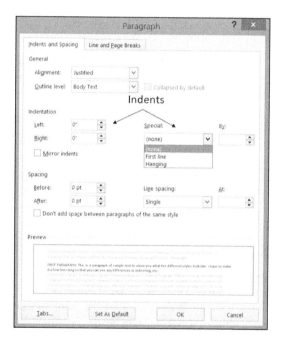

To indent the entire paragraph, change the value under Indentation where it says Left. To indent just the first line of a paragraph, choose First Line from the dropdown menu under Special and then select by how much in the By box. To have the first line flush left, but the lines below that indented, choose Hanging from the dropdown menu under Special and then selected how much those other lines should be indented by entering a value in the By box. (Usually .3 is a good value to go with, Word defaults to .5)

If you just want to indent a line of text or an entire paragraph, you can use the Increase Indent (or Decrease Indent) options in the Paragraph section of the Home tab. These are the ones that have four lines with blue arrows pointing either to the left (for decrease indent) or the right (for increase indent). You can also use tab (to indent) and shift + tab (to decrease an indent).

The problem with the increase indent/decrease indent menu options or the tab keys is in how Word records this for your paragraph format. For example, I just took a single word and indented it using the tab key. Word interpreted this as me wanting that paragraph to be formatted as having a First Line indent of .5". When I instead used the increase indent option on that single word of text, Word interpreted it as Left Indentation of .5". If it's just one line of text, it doesn't matter. But when you're dealing with an entire document, these little discrepancies can become a nightmare.

For bulleted and numbered lists, if you want to move an entire list further to the right or further to the left, select the entire list and then use either the Paragraph dialogue box, the shift or shift + tab keys, or the increase or decrease indent options from the Paragraph section of the Home tab to move it. The Paragraph dialogue box will give you the most control. The tab and shift + tab keys are probably the easiest to use. You can also right-click and choose Adjust Line Indents.

(If you choose Adjust Line Indents, you can also adjust the space between the number and the text by changing the Follow Number With option. This can be very useful when you have a numbered list that gets into the double digits.)

SPACING BETWEEN PARAGRAPHS

If you choose to style your paragraphs as left-aligned with no first line indent, you're going to need space between your paragraphs. The default style in Word is set up this way. You'll see that as you hit enter for a new paragraph that there's space left between the old paragraph and the new one.

If that space isn't present, you may be tempted to create one by using the enter key. Don't. It will mess with your formatting in a larger document as those spaces you've entered end up at the top or bottom of your pages. It's better to instead format your paragraphs to include the space.

You can do this by selecting your paragraph(s) and going to the Paragraph section of the Home tab. Click on the arrow next to the Line and Paragraph Spacing image (the lines with two blue arrows on the left-hand side, one pointing upward, one pointing downward), and choose Add Space Before Paragraph. In my version of Word that adds a 12 point space before the selected paragraphs.

If you want more control over the spacing around your paragraphs, right-click in your document and choose Paragraph to bring up the Paragraph dialogue box. The third section of the Indent and Spacing tab covers Spacing. On the left side you can see options for Before and After with arrows up and down. You can either type in a spacing value or you can use the arrows to choose the value you want.

If you set your paragraphs to have spacing both before and after, the space between two paragraphs will be the higher of those two values not the combination of them. (So if you say 12 point before and 6 point after, the spacing between them will be 12 point not 18 point.)

If you just wanted spacing at the top of a section of paragraphs or at the bottom of a section of paragraphs, you can click the box to say don't add spacing to paragraphs of the same style. Or just add paragraph spacing to that top-most or bottom-most paragraph. Usually this will come into play when you're dealing with a numbered list and want to separate it from the paragraphs of text above and below, but don't want that separation within your list.

If you don't want a space that is there, you can choose Remove Space After Paragraph from the dropdown in the Paragraph section of the Home tab. If you use this method, just be sure you've selected the correct paragraph (the one before the space you want to remove). Or, you can open the Paragraph dialogue box and change the paragraph spacing values for before and after to zero.

(Paragraph spacing is one of those issues that can become a nightmare in a large document where multiple users have been making edits. This is where sometimes using Format Painter to get the spacing between paragraphs consistent can be a lifesaver.)

OTHER FUNCTIONS

We've talked about how to enter text into Word and how to format that text once you've entered it and how to format your paragraphs. But there are a few more basics we need to cover that don't really have anything to do with entering or formatting your text, although they may lead to changes in your text.

Let's start with Find and Replace.

FIND

If you want to find a particular word or phrase in a Word document and you don't want to scan through the whole document, you'll need to use Find. It's very easy.

There are a few ways to do it (as is the case with most of the older functions in Word).

First, you can type Ctrl + F. In earlier versions of Word this would've brought up the Find and Replace dialogue box. In newer versions of Word this may instead just take your cursor to the Navigation search box on the left-hand side of the screen. If all you're looking for is a simple word or phrase, type it into the search box.

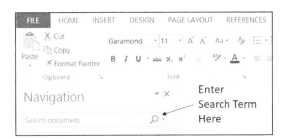

(Depending on how your document is set up, that search box may already be there for you to use. It is in my current document.)

Once you type a word into the search document box, Word will highlight that word or phrase throughout your document and tell you just below the search box how many total results there were. You can either scan through the document for all highlights of your search term or use the arrows next to the number of results to find the matches.

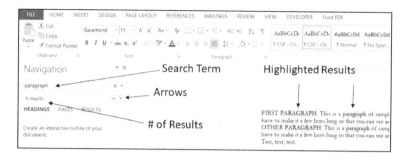

If you click on RESULTS directly under the search box, Word will show you a small snippet of each result on the left-hand side of the screen. In larger documents when you're looking for a very specific usage, scanning the results list can save time. For example, in this document when I just searched for "word" there were 92 matches. It's easier to look at the results list than scan through a thirty page document to look at each highlighted result.

To close your search, just click on the X next to the search term or hit Esc.

Another way to initiate Find is to go to the Editing section of the Home tab (on the far right) and click on Find from there.

But Find is more powerful than this basic search. You can do an Advanced Find that searches by formatting or limits your search results based on various criteria. To do that, you need to bring up the Find and Replace dialogue box.

One way to do so is to go to the Editing Section of the Home tab and click on the small black arrow next to Find. From the dropdown menu select Advanced Find. (Another way to do so is to type Ctrl +H and then click on the Find tab of the Find and Replace dialogue box.)

At first the Find tab doesn't look much more interesting than a basic search. That is until you click on the More option at the bottom left corner, which brings up a number of different search options.

Two of the most important options I use are "Match Case" and "Find Whole Words Only".

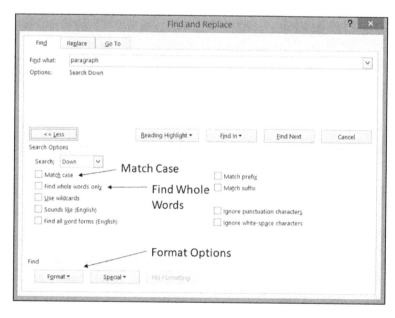

Match Case will look at the search term you enter and only find words with the same capitalization. So if you search for "CAT" and you check this box it will only locate "CAT" for you. If you didn't check this box, it would also locate "cat". (In this case CAT stands for consolidated audit trail and cat is an animal.) When searching for a proper name or an abbreviation like that, I recommend always checking this box.

Find Whole Words Only will only search for the entire word you enter. So again, with the example of "CAT", if you just searched Word normally it would return any word that has "cat" in it. So "category" and "implication" would be returned along with "CAT" and "cat."

Using Match Case and Find Whole Words saves you time when used with Find, but they can be vitally important when used with Replace.

Those are the only two options I use of the ones listed in that section. I can envision how some of the others would be useful, but I've ever needed them in twenty-plus years of using Word. What I have used is the Format option in the bottom left corner. If you click on that it will bring up a dropdown menu of options. One of them is Font.

Clicking on Font will bring up a Find Font dialogue box where you can specify the formatting you want to search for. In the screenshot below, I've chosen to find all text in italics. You can see it selected in the Find Font dialogue box and after I clicked on OK it was added under my search term.

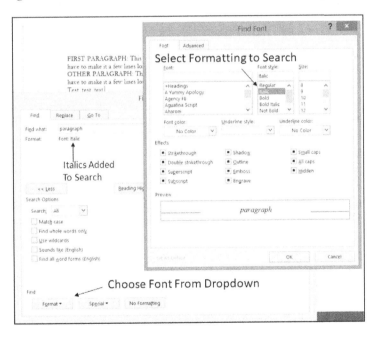

To find all italic text in the document, leave the search term box blank. When you click on search Word will show you all of the italic text in your document. This works for any type of formatting you want to find in your document and is good for combinations of formatting.

If all you want is to find text in italics (or text that's bolded or underlined), another way to do this is to click into the search box and then use the control key shortcuts. Typing Ctrl + I once will change the search so that you're looking for italicized text. Typing it another time will change the search so that you're looking for text that isn't in italics. Typing it a third time will remove it from the search.

Be careful when using the formatting search options that you don't forget to change an option and end up missing a search result you wanted to see. (For example, leaving it with no italics when you want all instances of a certain word, even those in italics.)

One last point. If you click on Special at the bottom of the Find and Replace dialogue box you'll see a list of special characters or attributes that you can also search on such as tabs and em dashes.

REPLACE

Find is useful. Replace is fantastic.

I have a bad habit with my novels of deciding after the novel is written that a character name needs to be changed. For example, I had a 90,000-word novel with a medic whose name was Marian. After reading Medic Marian one too many times I decided she needed a new name. But manually changing it would've been a nightmare. Find and Replace took care of it in less than a minute.

Same with fixing two spaces after a period. That's how I was taught to do things in school, so it's instinct by now. But there's a lot of negativity towards using two spaces after a period in the writing community, so now when I finish writing a piece I use find and replace to replace all instances of two spaces with one. I get to type the way I'm used to and I also get to deprive those judgey judgey types an opportunity to be nasty. Win win.

Having said that…

It's easy to mess up find and replace. Usually by not thinking through the implications of the changes you're going to make. Like in the example we had above with CAT. Let's say your boss wants you to replace all uses of CAT with consolidated audit trail. So you do. You do a quick find and replace for CAT and think you're done. Problem is, if you didn't think this through and use Find Whole Words Only and Match Case you also just replaced the "cat" in implication with "consolidated audit trail." Now you have a place somewhere in your document that reads "impliconsolidated audit trailion." Hopefully you'd catch that in spellcheck. But you wouldn't catch an instance where you replaced "cat", meaning the animal, with consolidated audit trail. You'd have some very confused readers when they reached the point where the firemen rescued the consolidated audit trail from the tree.

(I know. That's ridiculous and would never happen. But other things like that have happened.) Not what you want.

So the basics. To find text (or formatting) in your document and replace it, you can use Ctrl + H to bring up the Find and Replace dialogue box or you can go to the Editing section of the Home tab and click on Replace.

What you'll see is a Find What box and a Replace With box. In the Find What box type what you want to find. In the Replace With box type what you want to replace it with. So when I'm hunting down double spaces after a period I click into the Find What box and type two spaces and then click into the Replace With box and type a single space. Next, I click on Replace All and Word replaces all of the two spaces in the document and tells me how many replacements it made.

If you want to be more careful about what you're replacing, you can instead click on Replace. Word will locate the next instance of what you told it to find and highlight it. Click Replace again to replace the text that's highlighted with what you told it to use for the replacement. Word will do so and then go on to the next instance. If you don't want to replace that one, click on Find Next until you do find an instance you want to replace. When you do, click on Replace.

As with Find, you have the More option that lets you find whole words, match the case of your search term, and search by formatting.

Here's an example of a find/replace where I'm looking for instances of "paragraph" that aren't in italics and replacing them with "paragraph" in italics.

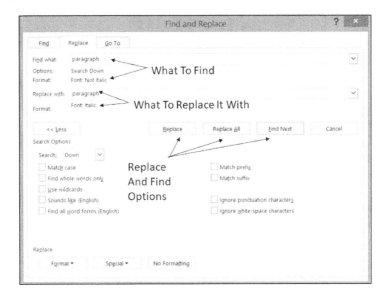

One other item to note. When Word does the find and replace, it will sometimes do so only from where you are in the document forward. When this happens it tells you how many items it found and replaced and then asks if you want to continue searching from the beginning. To be sure that you've found all instances, say yes.

SPELLING AND GRAMMAR CHECK

Unless you've done something to your settings or are working in a document that's already hundreds of pages long, you'll notice little red and blue squiggly lines appear under some words as you type. This is Word's real-time spelling and grammar check at work.

> As with Find, you can also fine-tune your search by clicking on More. This is where Match Case and Find Whole Words Only are incredibly powerful. No accidentally replacing all instances of "tom" with "bill" including changing "tomorrow" into "billorrow."

In the image above, there's a red squiggly line under "billorow" because that's not a real word, so Word identified it as a misspelling. The blue squiggly line under "More" is there because Word thinks that's a potential grammar error since I have a word capitalized in the middle of a sentence.

For spelling errors, you can right-click on the word and Word will suggest possible spellings if you're close enough to the actual spelling for it to guess the word. For grammar errors, it'll suggest the fix as well, but I usually leave those until the end when I run Spelling and Grammar check on the entire document.

The Spelling & Grammar check can be found in the Review tab on the left side in the Proofing section.

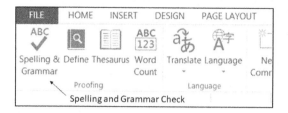

Once you click on it, Word will walk its way through your entire document checking for spelling and grammar issues. When it finds one it will display on the right side of the screen the issue it found and what it suggests as possible ways to fix it. You can ignore the suggestion, agree to the suggestion (by clicking on Change), or click into the document and type in your own edit to fix the issue.

With spelling errors, you can also choose to Ignore All if this is a word that's used repeatedly throughout the document but is not an error. (Like a made-up name or industry abbreviation.) In the alternative, you can choose to Change All if you think this is an error you've made more than once and you trust that there's never a time the word was used that doesn't need changed.

As you can see below, with spelling errors sometimes Word gives you multiple alternative words to choose from. Be sure you click on the correct one before selecting Change.

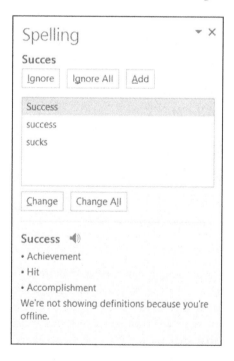

A word of caution when using the spelling and grammar check: Word is very good with spelling errors. It's not so good with grammar issues. More than once it has suggested the wrong version of its and it's to me. And it often fails to parse complex sentences properly, so ends up suggesting me instead of I when it shouldn't. You can read the explanations it gives, but don't assume that just because Word flagged a potential grammar error that it's right. Do not use it blindly. You will introduce errors into your document if you do.

When Word finishes with the spelling and grammar check it will display a Readability Statistics dialogue box. I sometimes find it interesting to know what grade level I've written to, but it's mostly useless for day-to-day purposes. Just close it out.

Also, once you've run spellcheck on a document and told Word to ignore spelling or grammar errors, it will continue to do so in that document. To run a clean spelling and grammar check of your document, go to the File tab and click on Options. Next, click on Proofing and click on the gray box labeled Recheck Document. This will show you a notice that you're about to reset the spelling and grammar check. Click OK. Now when you look at the document all spelling and grammar errors will be shown once more and when you run the spelling and grammar check it will show you everything it considers a spelling or grammar error.

WORD COUNT

One piece of information that can be useful in that Readability Statistics dialogue box is the word count of your document. Some short story markets, for example, have word count limits and some online forms restrict you to a certain number of characters. To see how many characters or words are in your document (or in a selection from your document), go to the Proofing section of the Review tab and choose Word Count. You'll now see the Word Count dialogue box which tells you the number of words, number of characters, and number of characters without spaces for your document or selection.

Your current word count is also usually visible in the bottom left corner of your document.

PAGE FORMATTING

We talked about how to format individual text and how to format paragraphs, but we still need to cover how to format a page. This is more relevant for when you want to print a document, which is why I saved it until this point.

PAGE NUMBERING

If you're going to print your document, you'll likely want to number the pages in the document. DO NOT do this manually. Word will do this for you and by letting Word do this, you ensure that the page numbering isn't changed when you make edits to the document.

To add page numbers to your document, go to the Header & Footer section of the Insert tab and click on the arrow next to Page Number. This will bring up a dropdown menu that lets you choose where on the page you want your page numbers to display and then how you want those page numbers to look.

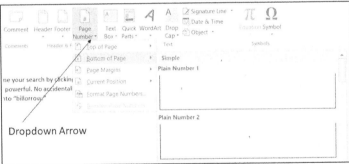

That should be all you need. Go there, choose Bottom of Page, Plain Number 2, and you'll have a document that has a page number centered at the bottom of each page.

In *Intermediate Word* I talk about how to create section breaks so that you have different page numbering in different parts of your document, but for basic, simple, page numbering you don't need to do more than I just showed you.

HEADERS AND FOOTERS

If you want text to repeat at the top or bottom of every page, then you should use headers and footers. Again, don't try to manually put this information into your document. One little change to your text and it'll break. (Not to mention how it'll look on an ereader.)

A header goes at the top of your page.

A footer goes at the bottom of your page.

To add one, go to the Header & Footer section of the Insert tab and click on the arrow below the one you need (header or footer), and then choose the option that works best for you, just like you did with page numbering.

You're not stuck with the format you choose. For example, with short story submissions, they usually want the header to be in the top right corner. If you choose the Blank header option, that creates a header that's in the top left corner. But you can simply go to the Home tab and choose to right-align the text in your header and that will put it in the right corner instead.

After you choose your header or footer option, Word inserts [Type here] into the designated spots where you're supposed to put text. To edit this text, just start typing because it will already be highlighted in gray. If it isn't, select the text and then start typing. Text in your header or footer works just like text in your document. You can use the same options from the Home tab to change your font, font size, color, etc.

Headers and footers are in a separate area from the main text of your document. So if you're in a header or footer and want to go back to the main document, you can (1) click on Close Header and Footer in the menu bar, (2) hit the Esc key on your keyboard, or (3) double-click on the main text in your document which will be grayed out while you're in the header or footer.

If you're in your main document and want to open a header or footer, you can (1) double-click on the text in the header or footer, or (2) right-click on the header or footer and choose "Edit Header" or "Edit Footer" from the dropdown options. I've found in recent versions of Word that double-clicking when there's just a page number in the footer doesn't work well for me and that I have to right-click and choose Edit Footer instead. This was not true of older versions of Word.

MARGINS

Margins are the white space along the edges of your document. The default in my version of Word is one-inch margins all around which is what most submission guidelines I've seen require, so you usually won't need to edit these. But in case you do…

(Because it looks like at least in Word 2003 the margins were not one inch all around.)

Go to the Page Layout tab and under the Page Setup section click on the dropdown under Margins. You will see some standard choices to choose from or the option at the bottom to set custom margins. If you click on Custom Margins, it will take you to the Page Setup dialogue box where you can specify the margins for top, bottom, left, and right.

You can also open the Page Setup dialogue box directly by clicking on the expansion arrow for the Page Setup section.

PAGE ORIENTATION

A standard document has a page orientation of portrait. That's where the long edge of the document is along the sides and the short edge is across the bottom and top. This is how most books, business reports, and school papers are formatted, and it's the default in Word.

But sometimes you'll create a document where you need to turn the text ninety degrees so that the long edge is at the top and bottom and the short edge is on the sides. A lot of tables in appendixes are done this way. And presentation slides are often this way. That's called landscape orientation.

(Think paintings here. A drawing of a person—a portrait—is taller than it is wide. A drawing of a mountain range—a landscape—is wider than it is tall.)

To change the orientation of your document, go to the Page Setup section of the Page Layout tab, click on the arrow under Orientation, and choose the orientation you want.

(If you use section breaks--which are covered in *Intermediate Word*—you can set the page orientation on a section-by-section basis. But if you're not using sections changing the orientation on any page will change the orientation of the entire document.)

PRINTING

Printing in Word, at its most basic, is incredibly easy. You can simply type Ctrl + P or go to File and choose Print from the list of options on the left-hand side. Both options will bring you to the Print screen.

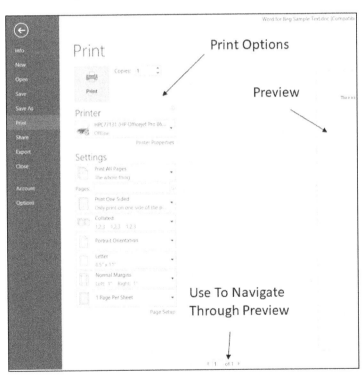

On the right-hand side you can see what the document will look like when it prints. For documents that are longer than a page, you can use the arrows at the bottom to navigate through the document preview. If everything looks good, you can just click on the Print icon.

But there are some changes you can make at this stage, so let's walk through them.

COPIES

Right next to the Print icon you can specify the number of copies of the document you want to print. The default is one copy. To increase that amount, either type a new number into the box or use the arrows on the right-hand side.

PRINTER

Your default printer should already be showing under the printer option. Sometimes I will change this to print to Microsoft XPS Document Writer or, if I'm working on a corporate computer, a PDF. This is for when I don't want to print a physical copy of the document but would like to have a version that can't be easily edited. (You can also use Save As to create a PDF version.)

SETTINGS: PRINT ALL PAGES OR PAGES

Below the printer choice are all the Settings options. In the Print All Pages and Pages section just below it you can choose to print just a subset of the pages in your document. For example, sometimes I just want to print one section or one page of a document.

You can choose from the dropdown to print the current page, print text that you've selected (print selection), only print odd pages, or only print even pages.

In the Pages box you can list individual page numbers that you want to print. For page ranges, use a dash. For a list of individual pages, use commas. So if you want to print pages 3, 5, and 7 you would enter "3,5,7" in the Pages box. If you wanted to print pages 3 *through* 7, you would enter "3-7" in the box. When you enter a page range in the Pages box it changes the dropdown menu to "Custom Print."

SETTINGS: PRINT ONE-SIDED OR TWO-SIDED

The default is for Word to print on one side of the page, but you can change it to print two-sided documents. To do so, click on the arrow next to the default choice of one-sided. You'll now see a dropdown with four options, one-sided, both sides with the long edge, both sides with the short edge, and manually print on both sides.

Choose the manual option if you have a printer that isn't set up to print two-sided documents.

Choose to flip pages on the long edge for documents with a portrait orientation. (This will be most documents.) Choose to flip pages on the short edge for documents with a landscape orientation.

SETTINGS: COLLATION

This is only relevant if you're printing more than one copy of a document that's more than one page long.

The default when printing multiple copies of a document is to print one entire copy of the document and then print the next copy of the document. (That's the collated option that shows 1,2,3 and then 1,2,3.)

The other option you can choose is to print all of your page ones and then all of your page twos and then all of your page threes. (That's the uncollated option that shows 1,1,1 and 2,2,2, etc.) The uncollated option is useful for situations where you might be giving out handouts one page at a time, but generally you'll want to stick with collated copies.

SETTINGS: ORIENTATION

We talked about this one before, but if you want the text on your page to go across the long edge instead of the short edge, this is another place where you can make that selection. The default is Portrait Orientation, but if you click on the arrow, you can instead choose Landscape Orientation.

SETTINGS: PAPER SIZE

The default in Word (at least in the U.S. version) is to print on 8.5"x11" paper. If you want to print your document on a different size of paper (say A4 or legal), then this is where you'd change that setting.

There are an insane number of choices both on the dropdown menu and if you click on More Paper Sizes but for most documents you'll probably be using the default.

If you do change the paper size, make sure that your printer has the correct paper in it.

SETTINGS: MARGINS

We already talked about how to change the margins on your document, but this is another place where you can do that. You have a list of pre-formatted options as well as the ability to customize.

SETTINGS: PAGES TO PRINT PER SHEET

If you want to save paper because perhaps you're reviewing a document and it's not the final version, you can print more than one page of your document onto a single sheet.

The default is to print one page on one sheet, but if you click on the dropdown menu here you can choose to print 2, 4, 6, 8, or 16 pages per sheet. You can also choose to scale your text to a chosen paper size.

Be careful with this, because Word will let you make a choice that results in an illegible document. Four pages on one is still legible, but I suspect that sixteen pages on one page would be virtually useless. (Unless you're in a situation where your teacher said you could bring one page of notes and you're trying to cram an entire semester's worth of knowledge on that one page.)

PAGE SETUP

As a beginner, I'd ignore the Page Setup link at the bottom of the page. Most of what it covers we've already addressed above. It's just the older way of specifying your print settings.

CUSTOMIZED SETTINGS

We're almost done, but before we wrap up I want to talk about how to customize your version of Word. I've already mentioned the Quick Access Toolbar, but there are some other settings I routinely adjust in order to get Word to work for me in the way I want it to.

Everything we're going to talk about in this section can be found in the File tab under Options with the exception of the last one which is found in the File tab under Info.

So first go to the File tab and from there click on Options. This will bring up the Word Options dialogue box (below).

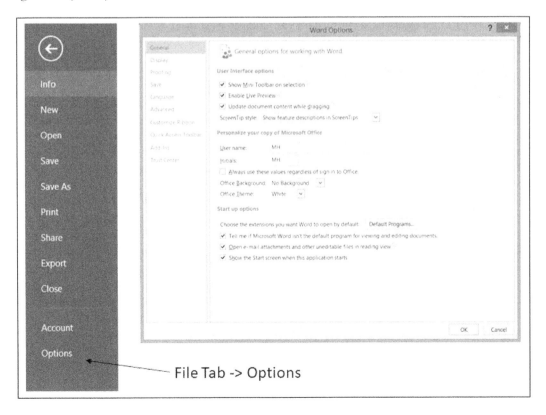

File Tab -> Options

If there's a setting in Word that's giving you problems, chances are the way to fix it is buried somewhere in this dialogue box. I'll walk you through a few key things I change, but you might find it worthwhile to explore on your own. Just be warned that any changes you make here will affect *all* of your Word documents, not just this one. So be careful.

(And if you're using someone else's version of Word and wondering why it looks so different, changes they've made here could very well be the reason.)

FILE -> OPTIONS -> GENERAL SETTINGS

This is where you can customize how your user name and initials will display for things like track changes, adding comments, and document properties. (None of which we've discussed so far but which you may run into if you're working on group documents.)

If you're going to change this, like I have, you also need to check the box that says to always use these values. If you don't, newer versions of Word that use your Windows login will override what you put here.

FILE -> OPTIONS -> DISPLAY

I'm pretty sure I've customized this one by clicking on the box that says to show white space between pages in print layout view. Without this box checked, you can't visually see page breaks in your document. One page of text rolls right into the next with just a thin gray line to indicate a page break. It's fine when you're dealing with longer pages of text or a report without breaks, but when you have very short chapters or sections, you can end up with three or four of them displayed on a single page. That annoys me, so I change it.

FILE -> OPTIONS -> PROOFING

This one I always have to mess with.

My former day job involves a lot of rule citations, where you write things like Rule 3070(c). Unfortunately for me, one of the proofing defaults in Word is to automatically convert (c) into the copyright sign. That's probably very handy for most of the population, but a complete pain for someone like me. So every time I get a new version of Word, I have to remove that one from the list of AutoCorrect Options.

In the other tabs in this section you'll find things like replacing straight quotes with smart quotes (which you're supposed to do for fiction writing). To get this one to actually change, you have to make that change in two tabs, the AutoFormat as You Type tab and the AutoFormat tab.

This is also the area of Word where I have a setting that converts typing two dashes in a row into an em-dash. (If you do this, you need to space after the next word to get the conversion to happen. And if the word is a contraction you actually need to space before the apostrophe to get it to convert. So dash, dash, word, space and you'll get —word but type dash, dash, word and you'll just have --word.)

A lot of the autocorrect options are very handy—I often type too fast and mistype "the" and Word always catches that for me—but do keep an eye out for "errors" you don't want fixed as you type.

It's probably a good idea to take a look through the tabs just to make sure there aren't any listed that you know you won't want to use.

This is also the section where you can create a Custom Dictionary if your company allows it. For example, my first name is always flagged by spellcheck. When I can, I add it to my custom dictionary so I don't get a spelling alert every time I send an email.

This is also where you can customize the settings for the spelling and grammar check. I usually use the default settings, but if you don't want to have Word flagging issues as you type, this is where you can turn that off.

FILE -> OPTIONS -> SAVE

In this section can specify how often Word saves a recovery version of your document. This can be a life saver if your computer or Word crash while you're working.

I always have autorecovery turned on even though it can be annoying. For some reason the CreateSpace templates take forever to save the autorecovery version. And the document freezes while it's doing it. But all it takes is losing something you were working on once to appreciate how important autorecovery can be.

You can specify here how often Word should save and where it should store that file. In newer versions of Word when Word crashes the next time it opens you'll be given the option of opening the recovered version and/or the last saved version.

If that doesn't happen, notice here where those files are saved. There's a chance that you may be able to go to that location and recover the file you need from there.

Best practice, though, is to make a habit of saving your files on a regular basis even if you're not done with them yet.

FILE -> OPTIONS -> ADVANCED

There are a ton of options in this section. I don't recall changing any of these in my own personal version of Word, but you might want to glance through to see if there's something you want to change. (And it's possible that I did change one of these a couple years ago and now just don't remember it. I'm used to Word working in a certain way and when it doesn't I usually go looking for a way to fix it or change it to what I'm familiar with. But with all the choices in File -> Options, you only need to change them once and then they're that way for that version of Word forever or until you change them back.)

FILE -> OPTIONS -> CUSTOMIZE RIBBON

If you want to get really fancy, you can customize the content of the tabs at the top of the screen. Say you want everything you think you'll use consolidated onto your Home tab or know you'll never need to use Styles and want to remove them, you can do it. However…

I would advise against this. Because your customization will only exist in your current version of Word. It won't exist on your IT guy's version. It won't exist on your best friend's. It won't exist on the version that everyone else is using when they answer questions on the internet. Which means once you do this, you're on your own. Other people won't be able to tell you where to go in your version of Word to make something happen.

And, the minute you upgrade to a new version of Word or start a new job, you'll be back to using the standard layout.

FILE -> OPTIONS -> QUICK ACCESS TOOLBAR

This is another location for you to customize what appears on the Quick Access Toolbar, and this one I do customize. I've added Select All, Breaks, and Format Painter here.

FILE -> INFO

If you go to the File tab and click on Info, there are a few more things you can do with respect to your document that you need to know about. I hesitate to tell you about this, because people using it have caused me more issues than I can tell you. But since it may come up and is useful to know about, I'm going to tell you. Just be careful with this one, please. I can't help you if you screw this up. Okay.

So when you work on a file in Word it stores a bunch of information behind the scenes including who the author of the document was. Sometimes, when you're going to share a document with a client or someone outside of your group, you'll want to strip that information out of your document and anonymize it to the extent you can. And if you've used comments or track changes in your document, it's a very good idea to make sure those are all removed before you pass the document outside of your team. (No one needs to see that back and forth you had over that paragraph on page five.)

The way you review your document for information you might want to remove is by going to the Info section of the File tab and clicking on Check for Issues next to Inspect Document, and then choosing to Inspect Document. This will scan your document for all sorts of things like comments, personal information, embedded documents, collapsed headings, etc.

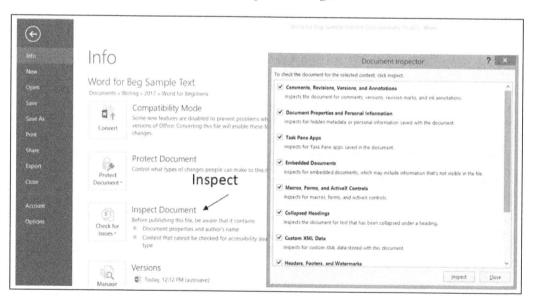

Some of this is very useful to check for. Some not so much. Like headers, footers, and watermarks. Chances are you wanted those in your document, so after you scan your document and Word offers to remove all of them, BE VERY CAREFUL. You can destroy a lot of work with just a click or two.

What I recommend if you're going to do this is that you save a copy of the file beforehand and then save the inspected and stripped down version as a new file. That way if you delete something you shouldn't, you can go back and fix it.

And always wait until the absolute end to strip out the personalization. I've been in situations where someone did this mid-review of a document and then everyone's comments on that document (and there were four or five of us providing comments) were listed as by Author. Believe it or not, that's a big deal. Because it matters whether that comment to edit something on page three was made by your boss or the new intern who doesn't know what they're doing but thinks they do.

So be careful. This one is useful but potentially dangerous.

CONCLUSION

Alright. There you have it. Enough knowledge about Word to let you do most of what you need to do. In *Intermediate Word* I dive into how to create complex numbered lists, insert tables, use section breaks, insert a table of contents, use styles, add watermarks and hyperlinks, deal with track changes, and more. Things that you may need to do at some point, but aren't essential.

If you found this guide easy to follow and want to learn that, then *Intermediate Word* is available for purchase. But there are other options. Now that you know the basics of Word, if you run into something you want to do but don't know how to do it, you can research how to do it either through Word or online.

First, within Word.

Hover your mouse over any of the options at the top of the screen and you'll see a basic description of what it does. For many of those options, at the bottom of the description is a question mark with the words Tell Me More. If you click on those words, you'll be taken to Word's built-in help function.

You can also click on the question mark in the top right corner of Word to bring up Word's built-in help function and then search for what you need to know.

I'll tell you, though. Nine times out of ten I search the help function in Word and give up after about a minute because what it says is nowhere close to what I need to know. But I always start there, just in case.

Usually, I end up doing an internet search for what I'm looking for using "microsoft word" as part of my search string. So I might search for "how to add a hyperlink microsoft word."

I then click on the result with the web address support.microsoft.com.

Bizarre as it is, given the general worthlessness of the built-in help function, the help provided on the Microsoft website is actually very good. If you want to know how something works, the website will almost always provide the information you need.

But it doesn't work so well with the "can I do X" sort of questions. (This is more often a problem with Excel than Word because there's only so much you can do in Word and it's mostly functional.)

If I have a "can I do X" sort of question, I do the exact same internet search as above, but instead of expecting an answer from Microsoft, I read through the top handful of results to see if anyone has asked my question before on a public forum and had it answered. Usually someone has.

If you still can't figure it out at that point (or even before that), you can also email me at mlhumphreywriter@gmail.com. I'm happy to point you in the right direction or figure out the answer myself. I don't check that email address every day, so you may have to wait a few days for me to get back to you, but I will get back to you eventually.

If all else fails, there are forums both on the Microsoft website and elsewhere where you can ask your question. Just be prepared for someone to imply that you're foolish or stupid for asking. I don't know why those types of forums are so obnoxious, but they are. It takes a bit of a thick skin to wade through and get the answer you need. Also, if you go that route, don't click on links from strangers. And be wary of anything that has you messing around in restricted files on your computer. It might work, it might break your computer.

Okay. So that's it. You should know the basics of Word at this point, and you now have the tools to find more answers if you need them. Good luck with it!

INDEX

CONTROL SHORTCUTS

For each of the control shortcuts, hold down Ctrl and the key listed to perform the command.

Command	Ctrl +
Select All	A
Bold	B
Copy	C
Center	E
Find	F
Replace	H
Italicize	I
Print	P
Save	S
Underline	U
Paste	V
Cut	X
Redo	Y
Undo	Z

ABOUT THE AUTHOR

M.L. Humphrey is a former stockbroker with a degree in Economics from Stanford and an MBA from Wharton who has spent close to twenty years as a regulator and consultant in the financial services industry.

You can reach M.L. at mlhumphreywriter@gmail.com or at mlhumphrey.com.